SOME HANDLIN'

BALLYRASHANE PRIMARY SCHOOL 1990

Photos Brian Webb

SOME HANDLIN'

THE DIALECT HERITAGE OF NORTH ULSTER

Collected by
Pupils and Friends
of
Ballyrashane Primary School

Illustrated by
Pupils of the School

NORTH-WEST BOOKS
1990

First published, privately, in 1986

This second edition published 1990 by
North-West Books
23 Main Street, Limavady, County Londonderry
Northern Ireland

BRITISH LIBRARY CATALOGUING IN PUBLICATION DATA
Some handlin' : the dialect heritage of North Ulster. — 2nd ed.
1. English language. Northern Irish dialect
I. Ballyrashane Primary School
427.9416

ISBN 0-907528-20-1

Printed by
Limavady Printing Company Limited
Catherine Street, Limavady, County Londonderry.
Telephone:- (05047) 62051

CONTENTS

FOREWORD

"Dialects vary not merely because of geographical separation or isolation but because each is in a fashion a reflex of the culture pattern of the community that uses it." Dialects are thus the mark of history (our own history) upon our tongues. If our distinctive linguistic roots are allowed to wither, a substantial part of our heritage withers irretrievably with them; our culture is diminished, becoming colourless and nondescript, difficult to distinguish from any other. Our Ulster linguistic heritage is unique, for it is a unique composite of a number of Scots and English dialects (mainly, though not only, of the west), with a sprinkling of Irish in those areas where Irish survived longest (the Sperrins, South Armagh, and the border areas). This rich variety of origin gives our dialect(s) a richness and variety of expression unparalleled in any area of comparable size.

It is a pleasure to commend most warmly the initiative and loving care with which Mrs. McIntyre and the pupils and parents of Ballyrashane Primary School have explored and recorded their local word-hoard, and gratifying to find not only much that is familiar but much that might have been thought to have disappeared. If our distinctive speech — the mark of a distinctive people with much to be proud of — is to survive, it must become more than a matter of sentimental recall and reminiscence among the old; it must be handed on by them in good health to the young as their inalienable birth-right, side by side with and enriching their standard speech.

I hope very much that others will emulate Ballyrashane Primary School and with equal success. Such local glossaries make an invaluable contribution to our projected Ulster Dialect Dictionary.

JOHN BRAIDWOOD

Late Emeritus Professor of English Language and Literature
Queen's University of Belfast

INTRODUCTION

Since the first edition of this book was compiled in 1984 there has been a perceptible change in attitudes towards non-standard dialect. Six years ago it was considered quite unacceptable in many quarters but now it is regarded as a distinctive aspect of our cultural heritage. In the consultation paper entitled 'Cultural Heritage : A Cross Curricular Theme' it is advocated that pupils should should know and appreciate a series of local words and phrases such as 'oxter', 'cowp', 'scundered', 'thrawn', 'forenen', 'carnaptious', 'a cup of tea in your hand', 'a face as long as a Lurgan spade' and 'do you mind the time?'

The first edition generated far more interest in dialect than we ever believed possible and it was this interest that enabled us to supplement what the late Professor Braidwood referred to as our 'local word hoard' with words from other parts of the province. Among the latter are words such as 'brength', 'clift', 'cub', 'etterecat', 'gabberlooney', 'sevendible' and 'sweeled'.

Some of the words recorded are contemporary and used mainly by the younger generation. These include, 'berk', 'bing', 'mingen', 'mooch', 'scrans', 'spoof', 'thrash' and 'wally'. At this stage such words are more slang than dialect, but over the years common usage will ensure that they become undeniably part of the Ulster vocabulary. Perhaps this is how dialect speech evolves.

Unfortunately a falling enrolment means that Ballyrashane Primary School will close within the next few years. Hopefully the success of this effort means that we will end with a bang rather than a whimper.

RAE McINTYRE

Principal, Ballyrashane Primary School
August 1990.

ACKNOWLEDGEMENTS

We at Ballyrashane Primary School would like to thank the following for their help:

1. Our parents, grandparents, neighbours and friends.

2. Mrs. Carson, the school cook, for explaining the meanings of words every time she was asked.

3. Mrs. Ann McIntyre, the caretaker, for supplying many dialect words.

4. People who lent us books:

   (a) Mrs. Hunter, who searched Coleraine library for books on dialect.

   (b) Mr. T. D. Johnston, Department of Education for Northern Ireland.

   (c) Mr. Stewart Love, retired librarian in the mobile library van.

   (d) Mr. James Richmond.

   (e) Mr. Trevor Scott.

5. Mr. Brian Webb, for the photograph of the school.

Thanks and appreciation are also due to the under-named pupils for the illustrations in this book:

Jacqueline Caldwell
Annabel Calvin
Gayle Carson
Lisa Gardiner
Ian Jamison
Alec Kearney
Lia McCloskey
Kerry Pettigrew

and to all the others who helped.

Slims

By Lia McCloskey

PART 1 : UNDERSTANDING THE DIALECT

A WORD-LIST

A

abane: above. *The roof abane our classroom leaks.*
airt: place. *What airt do you come from?*
aizel: cinder. *The toast was burnt to an aizel.*
allow: believe. *We allow that there will be another war.*
apt: certainly. *Did the dog bite Jacqueline? Middlin' apt he did.*
article: a very small person. *She is a bad wee article.*
ate: scolded. *When I got my trousers torn me mammy near ate me.*
auld: old.
a-waitin' on: very close to death. *He's just a-waitin' on.*
aye (1): always. *That wee boy is aye greetin'.*
aye (2): yes. *Are you going home? Aye.*
azoo: zoo. *The azoo is at Bellevue, outside Belfast.*

Birsey

B

bachle: silly awkward man. *A bachle walks as if he had two left feet.*

back return: part of a house sticking out at the back. *There was a new kitchen put in the newly built back return.*

badly done: embarrassed.

bagle: a small hound that gowls. A 'bagle's gowl' also means a distance away from something, a stone's throw. *She is not within a bagle's gowl of getting her work finished.*

bake: mouth. *I wish he would shut his bake.*

bap: small loaf or roll of bread.

barge: to scold. *She's aye bargin' about the mess.*

barm brack: a rich fruit loaf.

batter: road. *That man does a wild lot of visitin' and is never off the batter.*

beel: fester. *If you don't wash all the dirt out of a cut it might beel.*

beestins: a junket-like pudding made from the second milking of a newly-calved cow.

beetle: a gadget for mashing potatoes.

berk: a stupid person.

bings: many, plenty. *There were bings o' buns at the party.*

birces: anger. *Tanya's birces would get up very quickly.*

birl: whirl around and round.

birsey: a farmer.

blab: talk too much, tell secrets.

blabbermooth: someone who talks too much and tells secrets.

black neb: Presbyterian.

blether: talk nonsense.

blirt: weep.

blootered: very tired or very drunk.

blubber: sob.

bogey: hardened mucus in the nose.

boggin': filthy.

boke: vomit.

booch: hit or slap. *Me da hit me a booch on the jaw.*

boortreebush: an elderberry bush or tree.

boxty: fried grated potatoes and flour.

braid feet: large turf cut with a spade.

Quit yer blirtin' and blubberin'
Ye wud turn ma heid!

braird: new growth of freshly germinated seeds. *Thon grass seed takes a wild long time to braird.*

brattle: noise made by thunder. *Just after the lightnin' there was a wild brattle of thunder.*

bravely: well, feeling quite good. *How are you? I'm bravely.*

brength: Size. *Luk at the brength o' that wee cutty; she must ate a wild lot.*

bristlin': drying out potatoes boiled in their skins until they are toasted brown.

brock: rubbish, pig food, broken up.

broo: edge. *He cleaned out the sheugh and put all the glar on the broo.*

broughan: porridge. To 'spill the broughan' means to doze off. *Me granda nearly spilled the broughan after his dinner.*

bruckle (1): easily broken, fragile.

bruckle (2): cold showery weather.

buckies: wild roses.

bumfle: bulging. *His jumper was all bumfled up under his coat.*

burn (1): stream.

burn (2): ride on a motor bike. *Rhonda went for a quick burn on her Honda.*

C

canoodlin': kissing and cuddling.

cappy: a pet pig.

carnaptious: cross. *Teachers get carnaptious when we talk too much.*

cassy: a path. *There is a cassy through the farmyard to the fields.* (From "causeway", indicating a road or path with a stone base, (cf. French *chaussée,* raised part of a roadway)

cat melodium: terrible. *If our computer went on fire it would be cat melodium.*

champ: mashed potatoes with scallions.

chaw: insulting description of a woman.

chirm: whine. *Mandy is aye chirmin' about people annoying her.*

chitter: continuous talking. *We chitter all through dinner.*

chuff: please, make happy. *Stephen was all chuffed when he got a prize for swimming.*

chugh: tough. *Chugh meat is hard to chew.*

ciss: a long pointless story.

clabber: mud.

clachan: a small group of houses in the country.

claes: clothes.

claits: feet.

clap till: joined on to. *Robert's greenhouse is free-stan'in' and isn't a clap till.*

clarry: mess. *When a baby eats chocolate there is a wild clarry over his face, hands and clothes.*

clart: a very untidy girl.

clash: beat, hit, slap. *I hit him a clash on the lug.*

clatter: a large number of something. *Glenda's family owns a wild clatter of animals.*

cleek: hook. *My bicycle cleeked on to the fence.*

clemmed: cold and wet. *Alice was clemmed when she cycled home in the rain.*

clever: large, generous. *The woman in the shop told Mrs. Henderson that the blouse didn't have a clever cut.*

clift: a very silly woman.

clipe: tell tales.

clipe-clash: a person who tells tales.

clock: a black beetle.

THAT TEACHER
IS WIL'
CARNAPTIOUS

clocker: a hen sitting on eggs.
clod: throw. *Who clod the staipit cookie at Brither Gat?*
cloot: cloth.
clootie dumplin': a pudding boiled in a cloth.
close (1): secretive. *He was that close he could peel an orange in his pocket.*
close (2): clammy, humid, warm weather.
clouter: cough. *Nicola sometimes has a wild clouter.*
cockabundy: a gadget used to make ropes out of strands of hay.
cockaninny: a young girl with a very high opinion of herself.
coddin': joking. *Ah was only coddin' when Ah said you were as thick as champ.*
cog: copy. *We are not allowed to cog in tests.*
coggle: shake, wobble.
colf: to eat greedily. *Look at him sitting there colfing sweets into himself.*
collogue: a confidential conversation. *Claire and Sharmaine were having a collogue at lunchtime.*
collop: a slice of meat.
colly: specks of coal dust.
come-all-ye: a country song.
come-tae-me-go-aff-me: accordion.
comsleesh: an obsequious person.
cookie: a bun. A 'staipit cookie' is a bun dipped in tea.
coom: turf mould.
cooter: a long nose.
corbie: a crow.
cowp: tumble, knock over.
cowp-carly: turn head over heels.
crabbit: cross, irritable.
crack: entertainment, conversation. *We all have good crack at the swimming pool.*
craik: nagging continually. .*The teacher is aye craikin' about our writin'.*
craitur (1): a pathetic person.
craitur (2): whiskey. *A drop of the craitur is a glass of whiskey.*
cranchin': loud crunching. *Listen till her cranchin' sweets in church.*

Cockinanny

A young girl with a very high opinion of herself.

cratle: noisy breathing in the chest and throat; a death rattle.
creepy stool: a small three-legged stool.
creeshie: greasy.
crig: to hit one's bare toe. *I crigged me toe when I was walkin' roon in me bare claits.*
crine: twist. *In our classroom you have to crine your neck to look at the clock.*
cub: young boy. *There are mair wee lasses than cubs at Ballyrashane School.*
cuddy: horse.
cut (1): embarrassed or feeling hurt. *I was all cut when she insulted me.*
cut (2): drunk. *He drank a lot of whiskey and was half cut.*
cutty: a small girl.

Thon' wee cutty canny ride that pony

D

dander: stroll slowly. *I went for a dander across the cassy.*

dashlin: second-best clothes. *Daddy would never wear his dashlin suit to church.*

dead spit of: closely resembles. *Alec is the dead spit of his da.*

debble: wash clothes, usually by hand. *She was only debblin' out twarthy claes in the jawbox.*

deck: to punch someone.

dinge: dent. *There is a dinge in the bumper of our car.*

dinger: something going or doing well. *The new washing machine is going a dinger.* (Pronounce with hard 'g', as in "singer")

dinneling: vibrating, shaking. *She was dinneling the baby on her knee.*

dishabells: working clothes. *We change into our dishabells when we go home from school.* (from French *"déshabiller",* to undress or disrobe).

doitery: feeble. *The doitery old woman rarely goes out.*

doll: woman (usually "auld doll"). *That auld doll aye thinks folks are aye tryin' to steal her clothes.*

doncy (1): unwell, sick, dizzy. *Frances was very pale and she was feeling doncy.*

doncy (2): dishonest. *I look after my money when that doncy boy is around.*

dote: a pet, much loved child.

dozed: decayed, rotten. *The hot water bottle was dozed and it leaked all over the bed.*

dreech: dull, wet, dreary. *November days are often dreech.*

dribs and drabs: gradually. *Ann removed all the furniture from the old house in dribs and drabs.*

drookit: wet. *Clabber is drookit stoor.*

drooth: drying. *You wouldn't hang clothes out on a wet day because there would be no drooth.*

droothy: thirsty.

dughill: midden (dunghill).

dull: a loop or eye on a piece of string. This is used for poaching fish, particularly salmon.

dullin': poaching.

dulse: edible seaweed.

duncher: man's flat cap.

dunnerheid: silly person.
dunt: a thump. *When our television doesn't work I hit it a dunt.*
dwammel: a bout of sickness or dizziness. *Some children have a wee dwammel during Assembly.*

Hit thon television a dunt wi yer fut tae make it work

E

eejit: silly person.

een: eyes.

egg-nog: scrambled eggs (See Appendix 2)

elder: udder.

etterecat: a person who is very easily annoyed.

evening: afternoon. *The breadman usually comes at three o'clock in the evening.*

F

fadge: potato bread (see Appendix 2).

failed: has lost weight and is pale-faced. *Ian was badly failed after he had glandular fever.*

fanked: tangled. *Dan's fishing line got all fanked up in a tree.*

farl: a round loaf of soda bread usually cut in four (See Appendix 2).

fell: hit heavily.

ferntickles: freckles.

fissake: Hallowe'en mask.

fissle: light rustling noises. *The minister doesn't like it when we fissle sweetie papers in church.*

flaffin': flapping. *Robert's coat was flaffin' out behind him when he was ridin' his bicycle.*

flitters: rags. *The tramp's clothes were in flitters.*

flough: soft brown peats (not much good as fuel). (Pronounced to rhyme with 'cow').

fog: moss.

foggin': eating greedily. *She's sittin' there foggin' sweets intil herself.*

foggy: mossy. Often used to described turf.

foosty: musty, moulded.

footer (1) (noun): someone who is awkward and clumsy.

footer (2) (verb): to move about in an aimless fashion.

forbye: besides. *I have another coat forbye this one.*

forenenst: opposite. *The church is forenenst the school.*

form: condition. *John was in bad form when he had measles.*

fother: feed animals with hay.

founder: to be very cold. *It would founder you in our school during the winter.*

fozy: spongy. *Fozy peats burn up too quickly.*

frae: from.

frae-me-come-tae-me: trombone.

friend: relation. *Ellen and Amanda are friendly but they are not friends.*

frizzled: burnt. *Gayle like her toast frizzled to an aizel.*

futless: walking awkwardly as if you had two left feet.

G

gabbin': talking a lot.
gabberloony: a person who acts the fool and talks too much.
gabslick: a person who chatters all the time.
gag/geg: joke. *We have some quare gags on April Fool's day.*
gak: a foolish person.
galeery: silly, thoughtless.
gal: a piece of wood in a turf bank.
galluses: men's braces.
galoot: a silly person.
gamph: a silly person.
ganch (1): a silly person.
ganch (2): to talk stupidly.
gander: a look. *Take a wee gander at yon pair canoodlin' in the middle o' the road.*
gantin': yawning, fighting sleep.
ganzy: jumper.
gawk: stare.
gazaybee: a large useless structure. (From "gazebo")
geelgowan: yellow daisy.
geek: a weird-looking man.
geelig: earwig.
get on me: put on clothes. *I had to get on me very quickly after swimming.*
gettin': being attended to or being waited on. *"Are youse gettin'?"* is sometimes asked by shop assistants and waitresses.
gipe: silly person.
girn: whine, nag.
glam: to grab someone with your hands, to paw over them.
glar: mud, drookit stoor
gleed: sense. *He hasn't a gleed.*
gleek: a look. *Wee Lisa likes to take a gleek at her tables when she's doing Maths.*
glit: green slime found on damp walls, duckweed on a pond.
gleegid: senseless.
glouter: tapioca.
goamey: fool.
gobbler: turkey.
good hand: a witty person.
goosegabs: gooseberries.

Yon wee gabslick santers on all the time

Me sore finger is gopin'

gopin': throbbing. *My sore finger was gopin'.*
gorb: a greedy person.
gormless: stupid.
gornet: a kind of fish (a gurnet), a silly person.
gorry: a mess. *The tractor drove over the muddy field and made a wild gorry.*
gowf: slap or hit.
gowl: shouting, yelling, noise made by bagle. A bagle's gowl means the same as a stone's throw.
gowpinful: as much as you can hold in your two hands. (See Appendix 1).
graip: digging fork.
granny greybeard/granny mush-mush: hairy caterpillar.
great: very good friends. *Beverly and Shirley are very great.*
greesha: red hot ashes.
greet: cry. *She thinks it's Christmas all year round because she's aye greetin'.*
grist: guess, estimate. *Some women just grist weights when they are baking instead of weighing.*
group: channel in byre where liquid manure runs.
gub: mouth.
guff: cheek, insolence.
guid on ye: good for you.
gulder: shout.
gull: a person who stupidly believes everything.
gullion: a muddy hole.
gully: a large household knife.
gunge: sweets, cakes, desserts.
guniog: a slap. *Me ma gave me a guniog on the lug.*
gunk: disappointment. *We would have the quare gunk if we didn't get to the Isle of Man.*
gurly: stormy.
gutties: P.E. slippers.
guy: very. *She is guy stupid.*

Yon coo has a quare big elder on her
Aye the poor cratur's hefted

H

hack: tolerate. *We can't hack a week of wet lunchtimes.*

haenin': being frugal. *Between haenin and wantin' we'll get through.*

hag: to cut something up. *He cut himself when he was haggin' sticks.*

hair: the slightest bit. *The mother's a wild gossip, and the young cutty is no' yin hair better.*

half-tore: rather drunk.

hallion: clumsy boy.

hanch: big bite. *Lia's dog took a hanch at the sheets flaffin' on the line.*

handless: someone who is no good at making things with her hands.

handlin: an unusual situation. *Making this dictionary of dialect is some handlin'.*

hap: wrap someone up, tuck them in, in bed.

harlin': heaving. *Between pullin' and harlin' we'll get this thing moved.*

harned: hardened. *Oat cake was harned on a harner.*

harner: iron stand, set in front of an open turf fire, used in baking oatcake.

harry hunner feet: centipede.

haugh: shin bone used in making broth.

haveril: a slatternly woman.

heedrig: end of drills, where a farmer turns a tractor when ploughing.

head-the-ball: a person lacking in sense.

heart-scalded: vexed, annoyed. *We are heart-scalded with flies in the summer time.*

heel the begs: empty potatoes from a bag.

hefted: heaving and full. *The cows were hefted and needed to be milked.*

hersle: hurry. *She had to get herself hersled up to catch the bus.*

het: hot.

heth: certainly. *Would you sniff glue? Heth an' I would do not such thing.*

hidin': beating.

hinch: pelvic bone. *She rested the baby on her hinch.*

That Slurry is a wil' hoger

hinner: end, last days. *Johnny retired as church sexton at the hinner end of 1983.*

hirple: limp. *The boy hirpled because he had hurt his foot.*

hoachin: infested. *The dump is hoachin with rats.*

hooch: shout. *She gave a wil' hooch when she won first prize.*

hoger: a bad smell. *Slurry is a wild hoger.* (from French *haut goût,* well-seasoned)

hoke: search, dig. *The dog hokes through the bin for bones.*

hoof: walk. *He had to hoof it home.*

hoof-it!: Go away!

hooley: party.

howlt: an awkward situation. *David was in a howlt when his bicycle tyre punctured.*

hubble: fuss and bother. *Mrs. Carson got in a hubble when there was a power cut, and the school dinners weren't cooked.*

hume: bad smell.

hummins: small pieces of chewed food.

hungry: lean, infertile. Hungry land is very infertile.

hunkers: sitting on your heels.

huzzy/hizzy: a young girl.

I

ignorant: badly behaved, bad mannered. *He is as ignorant as a pig.*

insense: to explain, to make someone understand something. *The teacher couldn't get division insensed into his head.*

itchypoos: rose hips.

J

jap: splash. *My legs got japped with mud when a car passed me on a wet day.*

jawbox: a kitchen sink.

jeetled: very tired.

jeuk: duck down, avoid. *Nicola jeuked when her da was going to clash her.*

jeuk-the-beetles: lumps in mashed potatoes.

jibble: dribble, spill. *Tanya jibbled some tea on the floor when she was carrying a cupful.*

jing-bang: total (used for emphasis). *He ate the whole jing-bang packet of sweets.*

jinny: an effeminate man.

jip: extreme discomfort and pain. *I had toothache and it gave me jip.*

jip-job: something in bad condition. *The car was fixed after the crash but it was only a jip-job.*

joogins: pieces. *The dog chewed up the new shoes and had them in joogins.*

jorry: a small pet pig.

jube: guess. *Dan jubed that there was a big fish in a deep part of the river.*

jundy: shake or nudge. *Mandy gave Glenda a jundy on her arm and Glenda spilled her water.*

K

kale: cabbage.

kaleying: visiting in other people's houses.

katie hunkers: sitting on your heels.

keeho: a loud laugh.

keek: peep. *Amanda was keekin' in the window to see what her mother was doing.*

keenyin': whining. *The dog was sitting out in the rain and was keenyin' to get inside.*

kell: encrusted dirt. *The boy didn't wash his neck, and there was a kell right round it.*

kelled: muddy. *Ann gets cross when the boys come in from the football field with kelled boots.*

kepping: making cattle walk where you want them to. *Claire was keppin' the cattle so that they wouldn't go through the garden gate.*

kerfuffle (1): shake or toss.

kerfuffle (2): hug, kiss.

kitchen: a meal eaten with a knife and fork, something savoury. *We just had scones and tea last night and no kitchen.*

kitter-fisted: left handed.

kittery: cross, irritable.

kittled: had kittens. *The cat kittled on the bed.*

kittlin: a kitten.

knots: leaf or flower buds. *There are knots on rhododendrons all winter.*

kye: cattle.

The cat kittled on the bed.

L

lachter: a brood of chickens. *A hen has to clock on eggs for three weeks to hatch a lachter.*

Lambeg: a very large drum beaten with canes.

lammin: a beating.

lashins: plenty. *We get lashins of roasties in school.*

learn: to teach. *Me mammy learned me to tell the time.*

leather (1): to beat.

leather (2): ladder.

leggered: thick with mud. *The floor was that leggered in drookit stoor that the mop was black in no time.*

lend (noun): loan. *Give me the lend of your rubber.*

lickin' (1) (noun): a beating.

lickin' (2) (verb): currying favour. *She's always lickin' round her granda to get money.*

lift: arrest. *The police caught the man stealing and lifted him.*

lils: threadbare, torn. *The tramp's clothes were hanging in lils.*

lilty (1) (noun): a very bouncy, energetic woman.

lilty (2) (adjective): feeling full of energy.

line: main road. *There was a car accident on the Ballymoney line.*

loan: back yard.

loanin: lane.

lock: a number of something. *I could eat a lock of sweets just now.*

loggy: dull, warm, clammy. *On loggy days the humidity is high.*

look: want. *Beverly is lookin' a new schoolbag.*

lug: ear.

lum: chimney. *Long may your lum reek* (Long may your chimney smoke)

lythin: onions, flour and water fried in a pan (See Appendix 1).

On thonder hill there stood a coo
She's no there noo
She maun hae shifted

M

make: a penny. *He is so mean he wouldn't give you a make.*

march: pieces of land that are side by side, often in different ownership. *The school ground marches the manse ground.*

margiemore: an awful mess. *We make a margiemore when we paint.*

marley: marble (as used in children's games)

masters: end of school break. (Used only in Ballyrashane Primary School).

maun: must. *On thonder hill there stood a coo;*
She's no there noo,
She maun hae shifted.

mealie crushie: oat meal and onions fried in bacon fat.

measled: red and blotched. *She had measled shins because she sat in front of the fire.*

meat: all food. *Some hae meat and cannae eat.*

mell: thump.

mergeagled: twisted, tangled. *Sometimes the seat belts in a car get mergeagled.*

messages: shopping, usually meaning groceries.

middle shade: centre parting, in your hair.

middlin': feeling not very well. *Kara was middlin' after she had 'flu.*

mind: remember. *We all mind the day we went to the Folk Museum.*

mingen: rotten.

missly: badly missed. *The water supply was turned off and it was a missly thing.*

mitch: to play truant.

mizzlin': raining lightly. *You would soon be drookit the more it's only mizzlin', so put on your coat.*

moily: a cow that has been born without horns.

mooch: to play truant.

moochted: musty, mouldy.

morrow: swopping a day's work. *Farmer A works with Farmer B for a day and then Farmer B works for Farmer A in return.*

morrowless: things that do not match. *The silly wee lass was wearing two morrowless shoes.*

mortual: mortal (See Appendix 1).
moss: a bog where turf is cut for fuel.
mouth: silly person, someone who talks indiscreetly.

N

nadger: a young boy. *He's a quare cheeky wee nadger.*

nancy: an effeminate man.

narration: row, uproar. *He riz* (rose, started) *a narration when his new car was scraped.*

neb: nose.

nerd: silly, stupid person.

nick: condition. *The secondhand bike was in great nick.*

nippit: tight fitting.

nyafflin: eating noisily with your mouth open.

nyam: the noise made by a Ballyrashane cat.

nyerps: annoyance, something getting on your nerves. *Pencil leads breaking would give you the nyerps.*

nyinger: spittle.

nyirm: to nag or whine.

nyitter: to nag. *She is aye nyitterin' and chitterin' about her husband's smelly feet.*

nyuck: steal. *He would nyuck the hole out of a flute.*

He wud nyuck the
hole out of a flute

O

Och och an a nee o!: Oh dear!

oory: unwell looking. *The farmer sent for the vet because the cow looked oory.*

oxters: armpits. *He was up to his oxters in glar.*

oxter-cog: to lift someone under the arms. *The policeman oxtercogged the drunk man into the police car.*

P

pachle: a lump. Usually describes a useless person.

pancakes: drop scones.

pant: a great deal of talk.

pappit: a very tiny person.

peat coom: crumbled peat, turf mould.

pech: grunt. *He ate so much he was pechin'.*

peely-wally: pale and sick-looking. *Shirley is nearly always peely-wally now because of her bad tonsils.*

pet: unusual weather. *March 24th was a pet of a day because it was so warm.*

physogue: face.

picell: to move about inefficiently. *She picelled about so much it took her two hours to make tea.*

piece: a packed lunch, usually a slice of bread and butter.

pile: a large number. *There was a wild pile of people at the carol service.*

piling: snow starting to fall. *Snow was pilin' the afternoon before the big snowstorm.*
pintle: a small, annoying person.
pirty oaten: bread made with oatmeal and potatoes.
pismire/pishmowl: ant.
plastered: very drunk.
plout: boil. *Some people put the teapot on the hot stove to give it a plout.*
plouter: walk about usually with wet feet. *Me mammy told me to stop plouterin' in and out over her newly washed floor.*
plugher: cough.
plump (1): a heavy shower of rain, thunder shower.
plump (2): boil.
pogled: to be very tired. *We were pogled after doing P.E.*
poke: ice cream cone.
porans: tiny potatoes.
potted heid: minced pork.
powter: to potter. *He enjoys powterin' about his garden.*
pracus (1): a mess, usually of food on a plate or dish.
pracus (2): a bargain or even something for nothing. *She went to the jumble sale lookin' for a pracus.*
prog: to look for a bargain or something for nothing.
prugh: the same as prog. *She was aye prughin' through the old woman's house.*
puny: very pernicketty about food. *He was a puny wee article and ate very little.*
puss: sour expression on someone's face. *Look at her sittin' there, the crabbit wee article, with an auld puss on her face.*

Q

quare: very great
quet/quit: stop.

R

ramelgarry: a long senseless story.
rare: highly unusual, or eccentric (of persons).
rarin' to: eager, badly wanting. *We are rarin' to go to the Isle of Man.*
rawsiner (1): a large glass of whiskey.
rawsiner (2): a thump. *Stephen gave John a rawsiner up the jaw.*
redd up: clear or tidy up. *We have to redd up our classroom before we go home.*
reddin'-up (noun): a criticism of someone in his or her absence. *As soon as Mrs. McBlatter left the party the other weemin gave her a quare reddin'-up.*
reek: smoke.
ree-raw: bad temper. *The teacher was in a real ree-raw and hit all the children.*
reever: hit, thump. *He gave the other boy a reever up the jaw.*
rench: rinse.
reth: a snowdrift.

Many's a time Michael rusted at the school gate.

ribber: an apron made from a hessian bag worn to protect the clothes in farm work.

rickle: wobbly building. Also someone who is a 'rickle of bones' is extremely thin.

rig: a pig that is neither male nor female.

rightly: feeling well. *It took Ellen a while to feel rightly at herself after she was ill.*

rip: a cross bad-tongued person.

rippit: a row.

rit: edge. *The rit of the sky is the horizon.*

roasties: roast potatoes.

rodden: a road through a moss. The throat is called the 'rid rodden'.

rookied: wrecked. *The Titanic was rookied by an iceberg.*

room: the drawing-room or sitting-room kept for visitors is often called The Room.

roughness: plenty. *The farmer worked hard and had a roughness of money.*

runchy: tough, full of fibres. *Runchy turnips taste horrible.*

runt (1): thick stalk of a cabbage.

runt (2): root of a tree.

rusted: refused. *The boy was going to come in to school but he rusted at the school gate.*

S

sally: willow. *Some children are beaten with a sally rod.*
santer: to talk continuously about very little. *The way that woman santers on would turn your head.*
sark: vest.
sauncy: pretty, full of personality. *Sharmaine is a sauncy wee lass.*
sautlin': simmering. *The praties were only sautlin' on the stove instead of gettin' a good plump.*
scad: shadow, tint. *She dyed her hair and it had a red scad in it.*
scad-the-beggars: leeks fried in a pan.
scaldy (1): baby bird with no feathers.
scaldy (2): someone with very little hair or with hair cut very short.
scoot (1): squirt water.
scoot (2): diarrhoea.
Scotch convoy: walking home with a visitor to your house who then walks back home with you.
scour (1): a thick drizzle of rain.
scour (2): diarrhoea (usually in animals).
scrab: scratch. *The cat scrabbed me with her sharp claws.*
scraik: screech. The scraik of day is dawn or daybreak.
scrans: food.
scrapins: very thin and ill-looking. *After he had the 'flu he was away to scrapins.*
screwmoose: a tiny fieldmouse.
scraw (1): top layer of turf.
scraw (2): to scrape.
scud (1): to give a beating.
scud (2): to put the first layer of plaster on a wall.
scunge: gallivant. *He spent the whole day scungin' the countryside.*
scunner: to sicken or bore. *We would never get scunnered with sausages and chips.*
set: to let in conacre on yearly tenancy. *The man was too old to farm so he just set his land.*
sevendible: severe.
shankit: legged. *A lang-shankit person is very long legged.*
sharee dance: a supper dance (from French *soirée,* evening).

When the dog got at Anne's teddy bear its head, arms and legs were sinnery

sheddins: cross roads. *There is no motel at the Ballyrashane sheddins.*
sheugh: a drain or small stream.
shire: to drain water off. *Jane's granny shired the oatmeal when she was makin' sowins.*
shired: cleared. *Teachers enjoy quietness in order to get their heads shired.*
sickener: disappointment, something unpleasant. *Lia got a right sickener when she missed the bus to Belfast.*
simmet: vest.
sinnery: separated. *When the dog got at Anne's teddy bear its head, arms and legs were all sinnery.*
skeek: a pour of tea.
skelf: a tiny splinter of wood.
skelly: glance sideways. A skelly-eyed person has a squint.
skelp: slap.
skimpit: tight-fitting.
skite: slap.
slabber: to talk stupidly.
slag: to tease someone. *We slag Frances about her boyfriend.*
slake: to clean inefficiently. *She gave the floor a quick slake with a dirty mop.*
slap: a hole in a hedge used as an entry to a field.
slater: a woodlouse.
slavver: to talk with your mouth full of spit.
sleekid/sleekit: sly.
sleuter: a lazy, very unenergetic person.
slider: ice cream between two wafers.
slims: small griddle scones.
slip: slim young girl.
slipe: pull along. *When you slipe along the floor you drag your feet.*
slug: swig, quick drink. *He took a slug from the bottle of lemonade.*
smalicking: eating noisily with your mouth open.
smittle: highly infectious. *The trake can be very smittle.*
smur: a thick drizzle of rain.
smush: rubbish.
sned: to cut off. *The bad little boy sned the heads off the daffodils.*

Mammy I don't want to eat my stiraboot this morning.

snib: a Yale lock on a door.
snoken: smelling around searching for something. *The dog went snoken round the garden.*
snore: huff. *My sister took snore and wouldn't speak to me.*
snotter: mucus from nose.
snottery: nasty. *She got very snottery when I broke her bicycle.*
sooleymander: a slap or thump.
soordook: buttermilk.
soorlicks: sorrel leaves.
sowins: water that oatmeal has been boiled in drained (shired) and sweetened, then eaten as a dessert. (Probably from Gaelic *Samhain,* All Hallows Day, when sowins were eaten).
spalter: to stumble, walk awkwardly. *She spaltered over the slippery wet floor.*
spangs: legs.
spay-woman: a woman with second sight, a fortune-teller.
spelder: to pull muscles, to injure onself. *She fell down the ladder and near speldered herself.*
spittin': rain starting to fall.
spoof: to tell lies.
sprachle: to clamber. *The big man sprachled out of the low sports car.*
sprags: feet.
sprickled breid: rich fruit bread.
spricklyback: stickleback.
spulpin: mischievous boy.
squeezebox: accordion.
staipit: steeped. *A staipit cookie is a bun dipped in tea.*
starve: to make very cold. *It would starve you in Ballyrashane when the North wind blows.*
stashy: fancy. *She got herself all stashied up to go to the disco.*
steugh: smoke. *There is a wild steugh from my Granda's pipe.*
stiaghey: mixed-up food. *She mixed up her spuds, peas, meat and gravy and made a wild stiaghey.*
stime: a very small quantity. *The fog was so thick that we couldn't see a stime in front of us.*

Kerry was switherin' about which books to take out of the library

stiraboot: porridge.
stirk: a heifer or bullock about two years old.
stocious: drunk.
stock: edge. *She was sore in the morning because she had slept on the stock of the bed.*
stoon: a sharp ache or pain. *My ears were sore and some wild stoons came into them.*
stove: bad or strong smell. *He has the quare stove o' drink off him.*
strappin': big and healthy. *She was a fine big, strappin' lump of an agricultural Irish girl.*
striddle: to sit astride. *The Queen doesn't striddle her horse at the Trooping of the Colour.*
strone: a pour of tea. *She filled up my cup with another strone of tea.*
stroop: a spout. *A teapot with no stroop isn't much use.*
strunt: huff, sulk. *I hit my sister so she went off on a strunt.*
sturn: stubborn, wayward. *That's a badly behaved, sturn boy.*
sugh: slap. *Me mammy gave me a sugh on the lug.*
sweeled: probably means swaddled or wrapped in. *She was that sweeled in her jeans it's a wonder the zip went up.*
sweetener: a person who bids at auctions (to put the prices up) but doesn't want to buy.
swingle-tree: a wooden structure used to attach various implements to the harness of a farm horse.
swither: to be undecided. *Kerry was switherin' about which book to borrow from the library.*

T

taig: Roman Catholic.
take snore: huff or sulk.
targe: noisy fighting woman.
tartles: hanging pieces (often of hardened manure).
taste: a small quantity. *We had to stop and get a taste of petrol.*
tat: a small tangled piece of hair. *She cried when her hair was being combed because it was full of tats.*
thaveless: incompetent.
the day: to-day.
the devil: very difficult. *A leggered floor is the devil to wash.*
the more: even though. *Helen never misses a day from school the more she hates it.*
the morra: to-morrow.
thick: very friendly.
think long: to feel homesick.
thole: to bear. *I couldn't thole the pain in my tooth.*
thon, thonder: that, over there. *The church is over thonder.*
thrapple: throat.
thrash: a party where there is plenty of food.
thraw: to twist.
thrawn: twisted, stubborn. *He's that thrawn he never does anything he's asked to do.*
thresh: beat (by corporal punishment)
thristle: thistle.
throughother: messy and untidy.
till: to. *He told me till shut me bake.*
titchy: tiny.
tittle: walk in a mincing faishion. *She went tittlin' into the town on very high heels and a tight skirt.*
tober: settle, calm down. *The teacher has to tober us when we are noisy.*
toty: very small.
tove: boast. *He's aye tovin' about his big car.*
tovy: proud, stuck-up. *She is a tovy wee article.*
trake (1): a long tiresome walk.
trake (2): diarrhoea and vomiting.
trevalley: a long spiel or scolding. *The woman gave the butcher a big long trevalley.*

We had to stop and get a taste o' petrol.

Luk at that thaveless goamy go in'
tae church in his dishabells.

trig: spruce, neat.
trigged out: dressed in your best clothes. *She was well trigged out in her Sunday best.*
trinket: small drain.
trinnle: wheel of a barrow.
trokey: a slovenly woman.
trots: diarrhoea.
tryst: make an arrangement. *Lisa trysted her friend Gayle to meet her in the Leisure Centre.*
tup: ram, male sheep.
turf: fuel peat.
twarthy: two or three.

My heads turned, all them weans fightin'.

U

underboard: describes a dead person, in a coffin, not yet buried.

uppity: snobbish, having a high opinion of herself. *She's got wile uppity since she went to live on the Mountsandel Road.*

V

veshels: dishes. *It took the old woman a long time to wash the veshels.*

W

wally: a silly person.

want: need of psychiatric treatment. *There's a real want in him.*

water brash: a rush of saliva into your mouth that often happens before you are sick.

wean: child.

weather: the present time. *We are doing a lot of writing this weather.*

wee: very small.

weechil: baby boy.

weeks: corners. *The slobbers ran down the weeks of the dog's mouth when he smelled the meat.*

weelass: baby girl.

wersh: tasteless, insipid. *There was no salt in the dinner and it was very wersh.*

wet (of tea): to make tea. *Hurry up and wet the tay, for I hae a wild drooth on me.*

whaling: beating.

whammel: hit or thump.

whang: leather shoe lace or long thin strip of leather. *She wore her pen on a whang round her neck.*

whaup: curlew.

wheeker: something very large. *The rich man left the waitress a wheeker of a tip.*

wheen: a number of. *I ate a wheen of sweets after my dinner.*

wheesht: quiet. 'Howld yer wheesht' means to keep quiet.

wheezled-up: If you are wheezled-up you have bronchitis.

whid: hint, rumour. *There has been a whid that our school is closing.*

whinge: cry, whine.

whitteret/whittrick: stoat.

wick (1): useless. *The film was wick.*

wick (2): nerves. *Wet lunchbreaks would get on your wick.*

wild, wile: very

won: defeated. *Lily won Willie in the race.*

wrought: worked,/be employed by. *Johnny wrought till McCaughans all his days.*

Y

yella man: honeycomb toffee usually sold at the Auld Lammas Fair in Ballycastle.

yerkin: the seam from top to toe of a man's leather boot.

yin: one.

yinger: phlegm.

yo: ewe, female sheep.

youse: plural of 'you'. *The waitress asked "Are youse gettin'?"*

PART 2 : USING THE DIALECT

IDIOMS

That shopkeeper would **put his arm** *into you.* (take money from you dishonestly).
He's standing there with his **two arms the one length** (not doing anything useful).
Since she had measles she hasn't been **at herself** (has not been feeling completely well).
Since he got that new job he's rightly **at himself** (prosperous).

She was nearly **beside herself** *with grief* (in an extreme state of).
He **looks like a bled gander** (is very pale).
He wouldn't **let his bone go with the dog** (give anything away).
I wish he would **put another bush in the slap** (close the door).

Do you think I **came up the Bann in a bubble?** (I'm gullible).
Away and **catch yourself on** (be sensible)
She only gave the floor a **cat's lick** (a quick wash).
I've never **clapped eyes on** *her before* (seen).
She **cleaned his clock** *till him* (was extremely insulting to him).
That blouse has a very **clever** *cut* (generous, large).
He's that **close** *he could peel an orange in his pocket* (acts secretively or furtively).
The mother told the children to **conduct themselves** *properly at the party* (behave).

That wee girl is the **dead spit** *of her mother* (very closely resembles).
There's a **dirty drop in him** (can be very wicked).

The teacher was wild cross and **ate the face off me** *for talking* (scolded me severely).
Since his last illness he's very badly **failed** *(much thinner).*
There's more **fat on a bicycle** (he's very thin).
It was a warm day, and she was out **in her figure** (scantily dressed).
Look at her sitting there **the full of her coat** (wearing a very tight-fitting coat).

When I woke this morning my mother told me to **get on me** *quickly* (get dressed).
If I got a bad report me mammy would **go through me and out the other side** (punish or reprimand).

He's a **good hand** *at the story-telling* (very able).
They **took a hand** *out of him* (teased him).
He wouldn't do a **hand's turn** (any work).
This project on dialect is some **handlin'** (an unusual and time-consuming task).
She has **no hands on her** (is no good at doing anything with her hands).
Thon cub has a **good head** *on him* (that small boy is very intelligent).
My **head's turned** *by all them weans fightin'* (I am very bothered by).
The woman in the shop handled the cakes with dirty hands and my **heart didn't lie** *to them* (I had no interest in them, or enthusiasm for them).
I wouldn't tell her anything because she couldn't **hold her own water** (keep a secret).
He **called for Hughie and Ralph** (vomited).
He's a very **hungry-looking** *man* (thin and unhealthy-looking).

Hunger is a good **kitchen** (relish).

The teacher **learns** *us the meaning of big words* (teaches).
Could **I have the lend of a wee taste of soap please?** (May I borrow a small piece of).
His land **lies into** *our land* (adjoins).
As like or not *there'll be frost tonight* (probably)
She **lit on me** *like a ton of bricks* (scolded me severely)
I'm sitting here **on me lone** (alone).
When he died he didn't **look like himself** (death changed his features).
He **looked** *his cattle every morning* (inspected, checked).
He had a sprained ankle and couldn't **mark** *his foot* (stand with his weight on).
Her child fell and cut his knee but she never **mismade herself** (didn't bother herself).
I love sweets **the more** *they're bad for my teeth.* (even though).

Helen never misses a day from school the more she hates it.

I got slapped over the head of my wee sister

Her **mouth's so big** *she can whisper into her own ear (very indiscreet).*
She's very **down in the mouth** *because she's not going to the party* (depressed). *They never asked me if* **I had a mouth on me** (wanted anything to eat or drink).
He's always **putting on a poor mouth** (pretending to be poor).
He's a **sore mouth** *of a body* (very silly).

She thinks she's **no goat's toe** (she has a very high opinion of herself).
She's **no miss** (she hasn't much personality).
She's sitting there with her **nose up the chimney** (sulking).

He's bad-tempered, but it wasn't **off the grass he licked it** (he inherited his bad temper).
Prince Charles is married **on** *Princess Diana* (to).
When my sister got married my cousin and I were **on the wedding** (attendants or main participants at the ceremony).
I got slapped **over the head of** *my wee sister* (on account of something she had done).

I wasn't hungry, but I ate enough to **pass myself** (to be courteous).
It was long after his bedtime and he was near **past himself** *with tiredness* (in an extreme state of).
He went to the bathroom **in his pelt** (with no clothes on).
There isn't **a pick on her** (she's very thin).
She wouldn't **put herself out** *for anyone* (go to any trouble).
I heard that he had stolen money, and I wouldn't **put it past** him (think it incredible).

We vomited **rings round him** (a great deal).
He has a right **roughness of money** *about him* (plenty of money).
On Sunday we went a **run** *to Ballycastle* (a drive by car).

Some children thought the transfer was **wee buns** (easy).
The owner of the factory was a **well set-up** *man* (prosperous).
He's **not the full shilling** (in need of psychiatric treatment).
You're a **holy show** *in that coat* (ridiculous looking).

She asked me to come in and have a wee cup of **tea in my hand** (a cup of tea not set in a saucer, and often taken sitting beside the fire).

He likes **tea to** *his dinner* (a cup of tea to drink while eating his dinner).

She'll not **tear in the plucking** (she's no longer a young girl).

When he was staying at his granny's house he was always **thinking long** (feeling homesick).

She **thinks she is somebody** (has a very high opinion of herself).

He was **near to himself** *when he fell off the motorbike* (almost had a serious accident.

Would you like a biscuit **to your tea?** (with).

I **took my dead end** *at the child* (was very amused).

Get **tore in till** *that dinner!* (start eating).

He's wild **badly walked** (walks in a very ungainly way).

There's a **bit of a want** *in him* (he is not completely wise).

The cross woman **wiped the floor** *with her son when he came home late* (severely scolded).

SIMILES

as **black** *as your boot.*

as **cross** *as an auld cat.*

as **full** *as a goat.*

as **lazy** *as sheugh water.*

as **long** *as a Lurgan spade* (used of the countenance). Apparently the use of both "Lurgan" and "spade" is tautological; a "lurgan" was a long leg bone (the town is supposed to be built on land that shape), and this bone, in ancient times, was used as a spade.

as **mean** *as get-out.*

as **pale** *as a bled gander.*

as **thick** *as champ.*

as **thick** *as pirty oaten.*

as **thin** *as two yards of pump water.*

as **wide** *as Molly's dresser.*

Doctor - I hope you're getting enough fibre and fresh vegetables in your diet.

Patient - Och aye.
I had broughan tae
me breakfast,
scad-the-beggars
and champ tae me
dinner and mealie-
crushie and pirty-
oaten tae me tae.

PART 3 : HELPS WITH THE DIALECT

Appendix 1

WORDS USED TO EMPHASISE

buck:
1. *He's a silly buck eejit.*
2. *He is buck stupid.*
3. *He took a buck lep* (leap) *over the fence.*

clean:
1. *That sewer smells clean rotten.*
2. *I clean forgot to do my homework.*

fair:
1. *I am fair scunnered with work.*
2. *She fair ate up her dinner.*

heth: indeed *Will you come out in the rain? Heth and I will do nothing of the kind.*

mortual:
1. *I mortually hate rats.*
2. *Five of us mortually have Irish stew.*

powerful:
1. *That wee boy is a powerful liar.*
2. *Sometimes it is powerful cold in school.*

quare:
1. *It's a quare day for sitting out in the sun.*
2. *Sliced bread is quare'n handy.*

right:
1. *Isn't she the right eejit for dyeing her hair green?*
2. *You've made a right mess of your book.*

some:
1. *This book on dialect is some handlin'.*
2. *That wee girl is some reader.*

sore:
1. *He's a sore eejit.*
2. *That man is a sore, stupid fool.*

wild:
1. *It was wild quiet in church.*
2. *I am wild hungry.*

NAMES FOR FOOD

bap: small roll or loaf of bread.
barm-brack: a rich fruit loaf.
boxty: fried grated potatoes and flour.
broughan: porridge.
champ: mashed potatoes with scallions.
clootie-dumpling: pudding boiled in a cloth.
cookie: a bun.
dulse: edible seaweed.
egg-nog: eggs scrambled (no milk added) and fried in bacon fat in a pan.
fadge: potato bread, made with mashed potatoes and flour and baked on a griddle.
farl: a quarter of a large round soda scone baked on a griddle.
fry: an Ulster fry consists of fried bacon, fried eggs and fadge, sometimes with sausages, fried soda farls, tomatoes and black pudding.
glouter: tapioca.
goosegabs: gooseberries.
haugh: shin bone used in making broth.
kale: cabbage.
kitchen: a savoury meal usually eaten with a knife and fork.
lythin: onions, flour and water fried in a pan.
mealie-crushie: oatmeal and onions fried in bacon fat.
meat: all food.
pancakes: drop scones baked on a griddle.
pirty-oaten: bread made with oatmeal and potatoes and baked on a griddle.
potted heid: minced pork.
roasties: roast potatoes.
scad-the-beggars: leeks fried in a pan.
scallions: shallots.
slims: small griddle scones.
sowans (sowins): to make sowins, boil porridge, shire (strain) off the water, and sweeten; it is the watery part that is supped, not the oatmeal.
soordook: buttermilk.
soorlicks: sorrel leaves.
sprickled breid: rich fruit bread.
stiraboot: porridge.
yella man: honeycomb toffee.

Boys I love clootie dumplin' for me puddin'.

Appendix 3

PARTS OF THE BODY

bake: mouth.
claits: feet.
cooter: nose.
croon: crown.
een: eyes.
heid: head.
hinch: pelvic bone.
hinner end: behind.
lugs: ears.
mooth: mouth.
neb: nose.
oxters: armpits.
sprags: feet.
thrapple: throat.

Appendix 4

CLOTHES

claes: clothes.
dashlin' claes: second best clothes.
dishabells: old working clothes.
duncher: man's flat cap.
ganzy: sweater.
ribber: hessian apron for rough work.
sark: vest.
shoot: suit.
simmet: vest.

He's a quer good looking bit o stuff but look at the size o his hinner end

HOW TO BE RUDE

The following is a selection of words which can be used when it is intended to insult someone in dialect; please consult the main word-list for their meanings.

bachle
bagle
baphead
berk
blether
chaw
clart
clipe clash
comsleesh
cuddy
dunnerheid
eejit
footer
futless
galeery
galoot
gamph
ganch
gazaybee
gleegid
goamey
gormless
gornet
gull
hallion
handless
mouth
pachle
pracus
prugh
scunner
sleuter
targe
thaveless
thrawn

WILD LIFE

ANIMALS

screwmoose: field mouse.
whitteret/whittrick: stoat.

BIRDS

corbie: crow
jinny-wren: wren.
throstle: thrush.
whaup: curlew.
willie wagtail: pied wagtail.
yellow yorn: yellow hammer.

INSECTS

clock: stag beetle.
geelig: earwig.
granny greybeard/granny mush-mush: hairy caterpillar.
harry hunner feet: centipede.
pismire/pishmowl: ant.
slater: woodlouse.

PLANTS

benweed: ragwort.
boortree bush: elderberry bush or tree.
buckies: wild roses.
buhilon: ragwort.
dockens: docks.
geelgowans: yellow daisies.
itchypoos: rose hips.
soorlicks: sorrel leaves.

FISHES

gornet: gurnet.
sprickłyback: stickleback.

Appendix 7

DOMESTIC ANIMALS

bagle: beagle, small hound.
cappy: pet pig.
cuddy: horse.
dropped calf: newly born calf.
jorry: pet pig.
kittlin: kitten.
stirk: heifer or bullock about two years old.
tup: ram
yo: ewe

Appendix 8

WORDS FOR CORPORAL PUNISHMENT

Words for a slap*:

booch
clash
fell (hit extremely hard)
gowf
guniog
mell
rawsiner
skelp
skite
sooley mander
sugh
whammel

Words for a beating:

beefin'
bleechin'
clashin'
hemmerin'
hidin'
kibbin'
lammin'
leatherin'
lickin'
scuddin'
threshin'
whalin'

*The word "slap" itself is used in dialect to describe a hole in a hedge or an entry into a field.

Appendix 9

WORDS USED FOR ILLNESS OR ITS SYMPTOMS

ammonia: pneumonia.
brownkatis: bronchitis.
trake: diarrhoea and vomiting.
wheezle: wheeze.
yellow jandis: jaundice.

Appendix 10

WEATHER

bruckle weather: cold showery weather.
close: warm, humid.
dreech: dull, wet, dreary.
gurly: stormy.
loggy: dull, warm, humid.
mizzlin': raining gently.
pet: a pet of a day is a very mild sunny day in winter.
piling: snow starting to fall.
plump: heavy shower of rain. A thunder plump is a thundery shower.
reth: snow drift.
scour: a thick drizzle of rain.
smur: a thick drizzle of rain.
spittin': rain starting to fall.
starvin': extremely cold.
teemin': raining heavily.
there isn't an air: it's very warm and humid.

SOME OF NORTH-WEST BOOKS' PUBLICATIONS

North-West Books publishes books of special Northern Ireland interest, and here are descriptions of some of them. In square brackets are given for each the current net price (which is of course liable to variation) and catalogue number (to which must be prefixed 0907528 to give the full ISBN).

A strong point in our list has been the reprinting of old and proven books of local history. Among these has been Colby's **Ordnance Survey Memoir of Londonderry** (1837) [£29.95; 18X], a large and comprehensive work. Simpson's **The Annals of Derry** (1847) [£12.00; 090] is a notable resource book, consisting mainly of extracts from earlier documents and dealing in detail with the Siege. **The Ulster Clans**, by T. H. Mullin and J. E. Mullan, (1966) [£8.95; 031] traces the rise of the O'Neills and the dominance of much of north Ulster by the O'Kanes (or O'Cahons). McSparran's **The M'Donnell and the Norman de Borgos** (1828) [£9.95; 082] describes itself as "an Irish legend", but tells a lot about north Ulster both by its narrative of times well before the Plantation and by the author's comments written not long before the Famine. Boyle's **Records of Limavady** (1912) [£9.95; 155] recaptures the ordinary lives of the people of a Plantation town through the minutes of its Corporation. Wallace Clark's **Rathlin** (1971, but up-dated to 1988 for this second edition) [£7.95; 112] tells the story of this unique island lying between the coasts of Ireland and Scotland.

Two original studies have been published, both concentrating on Presbyterianism in the Roe Valley, County Londonderry. J. S. P. Black's **Speaking Yet** [£3.95; 074] tells the story of the country congregation of Balteagh, and shows the social conditions in which it was born. J. E. Mullin's **The Presbytery of Limavady** [£12.00; 163] details the history of each of the twelve congregations in the area, and is of great relevance to students of genealogy. In his memoir **Days That Are Gone** [£5.95; 023] Sir Patrick Macrory recaptures life in County Londonderry sixty and more years ago.

Other interests are also catered for. Richard Doherty's **Wall of Steel** [£12.95; 139] is the history of the 9th (Londonderry) Heavy Anti-Aircraft Regiment, which spent most of WWII overseas. Wallace Clark's **Sailing Round Ireland** [£8.95; 171] is a reissue of a yachtsman's standard companion. **From "The North Atlantic" to the "Crackerjacks"** [£7.95; 120] gives through its reproductions of time tables and through a commentary by John Conacher a picture of the L.M.S. — N.C.C. railway just before WWII, during it, and soon after it. **Map Portfolio of Northern Ireland** [£65.00; 04X] is a unique compendium, with all the new Ordnance Survey maps of the province at the 1: 50 000 scale presented in a fine custom-made binder. **Some Handlin'**, the treasury of North Ulster dialect compiled at Ballyrashane Primary School [£3.95; 201], is the most recent publication, for Christmas 1990.

All of these books are obtainable through any good bookseller. In case of difficulty they may be bought from North-West Books, 23 Main Street, Limavady, County Londonderry, BT49 0EP, Northern Ireland (telephone (05047) 22835); postage charges are payable for mail order despatches.